FILM AWARDS

THE MOTION PICTURE ACADEMY AWARDS . . .

buddy adler	1956 –	THALBERG AWARD
	1953 –	From Here to Eternity
	1940 –	Quicker Than a Wink
richard rodgers	1945 –	State Fair
		+ 1 nomination
oscar hammerstein II	1945 –	State Fair
	1941 –	Lady Be Good
		+ 5 nominations
joshua logan		– 1 nomination
paul osborn		– 1 nomination
alfred newman	1956 –	The King and I
	1955 –	Love is a Many-Splendored Thing
	1953 –	Call Me Madam
	1952 –	With a Song in My Heart
	1947 –	Mother Wore Tights
	1943 –	The Song of Bernadette
	1940 –	Tin Pan Alley
	1938 –	Alexander's Ragtime Band
		+ 37 nominations
ken darby	1956 –	The King and I
		+ 1 nomination
leon shamroy	1945 –	Leave Her to Heaven
	1944 –	Wilson
	1942 –	The Black Swan
		+ 13 nominations
lyle wheeler	1956 –	The King and I
	1953 –	The Robe
	1946 –	Anna and The King of Siam
	1939 –	Gone With The Wind
		+ 25 nominations
john de cuir	1956 –	The King and I
		+ 5 nominations
walter scott	1956 –	The King and I
		+ 2 nominations
paul fox	1956 –	The King and I
	1953 –	The Robe
		+ 11 nominations
dorothy jeakins	1950 –	Samson and Delilah
	1948 –	Joan of Arc
		+ 5 nominations
leroy prinz		(no Academy Awards given for choreography; for direction, short subjects . . .)
	1946 –	A Boy and His Dog

rossano brazzi has won Italy's highest awards: the NASTRO D'ARGENTO (Silver Ribbon) and the COROLLA D'ORO (Garland of Gold); and the highest foreign actor award from France, Germany and Yugoslavia.

THE DANIEL BLUM AWARD . . .

john kerr	1952 – Bernardine

o
o
out
el
Jones
ey
o
el

Roberts
Get Your Gun

d Sympathy

THE N Y DRAMA CRITICS' AWARDS . . .

rodgers & hammerstein	1945 – Carousel
richard rodgers	1952 – Pal Joey
joshua logan	1953 – Picnic
john kerr	1953 – Tea and Sympathy
ray walston	1956 – Damn Yankees
	1949 – Summer and Smoke

ment) . . .

OK AWARD

ULITZER PRIZE . . .

a michener	1947 – Tales of the South Pacific

THE LOOK FILM AWARDS . . .

buddy adler	1956 – ACHIEVEMENT AWARD
leon shamroy	1949 – Twelve O'Clock High
	1944 – Wilson
mitzi gaynor	1951 – Golden Girl

est" --

1956 – Anastasia
1955 – Love is a Many-Splendored Thing
1953 – From Here to Eternity

1956 – Picnic

AND "Famous Five" AWARDS . . .

joshua logan	1955 – Mister Roberts
leon shamroy	1956 – The King and I
	1955 – Love is a Many-Splendored Thing
	1954 – The Egyptian
	1953 – The Robe
	1944 – Wilson

and award-winners

south pacific's awards

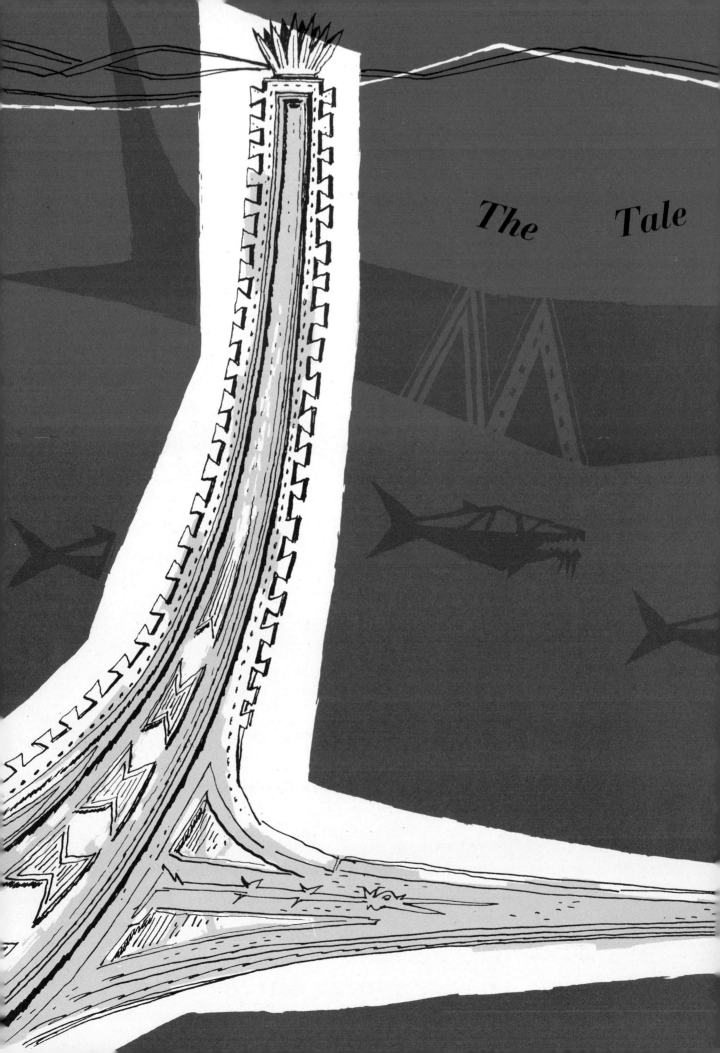

The   Tale

of

Rodgers and Hammerstein 's

SOUTH PACIFIC

This   Book

Edited and Produced by Thana Skouras

Designed by John De Cuir and Dale Hennesy

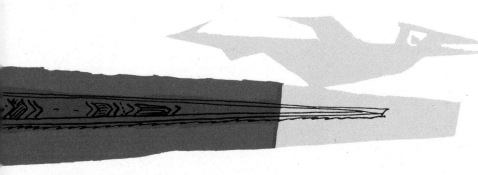

A Lehmann Book   New York   1958

FISHERMAN'S NAVIGATION CHART

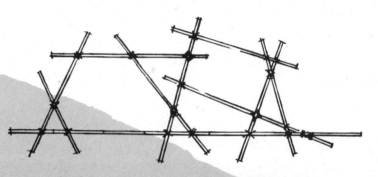

DERUJINSKY: Portrait Photographer
James Mitchell: Still Photographer
Gaston Longet: Associate Still Photographer
Rodger Maus: Designers' Assistant

United States of America by

Manufactured in the

the supervision of

and A Weinstein.

The United States Printing & Lithograph Company,

New York

under

John Lambie.

the word . . . . .

SOUTH PACIFIC

Toward the end of World War II, I
got one of the best breaks of my life. I was
stationed on a rear-area South Pacific island
where the commander, a good guy, was determined
to make an extra stripe. To insure his promotion,
he kept his roster as crowded as possible, so
that even though I had nothing to do I was
reported as absolutely essential. I complained,
but it didn't do any good because my commander's
boss was trying to make admiral--and he needed
all the people possible under him, too.

The system left me free to do pretty
much as I wished, on a remarkably savage yet
lovely island. I had as my assistants a wonderful Tennessee shoemaker named Jim, a cocky
little Los Angeles Mexican named Garcia, and a
worldly-wise Maine storekeeper named Morrison.
To them I turned over all my naval responsibili-
ties and the use of my jeep at night. It was
little Garcia who thought up the idea that kept
me out of trouble. Whenever anyone asked for me,
he replied, "Mr Michener is on the other side
of the island...on important business."

Actually, my days were invariable.
After handling all business routines in fifteen
minutes, I got into the jeep and explored my
island. I traveled with the medical man who
cared for the native children. I spent long
hours in the bar at the submarine base. I flew
with hot-shot pilots from the airfields. I
became good friends with the Catholic priest who
looked after a noticeably free-living and free-
loving French community. And I took long trips
both into the jungle and across the South
Pacific seas to remote islands.

On one such trip I happened to
stumble upon the idyllic set-up that some naval
officers at CASU-10 had built in the heart of
the jungle, on the property of Madame Gardel.
Through the simple process of stealing every-
thing that wasn't nailed down--refrigerators,
generators, canned food, beer, soda fountains,
and plush furniture intended for officers' clubs
--CASU-10 had constructed a magnificent night
club, complete with orchestra, catering service,
and gushing bar. And all within a few miles of
the war!

In later years, after I had written
a book about this island called Tales of the
South Pacific, a lot of military people gave me

hell for having described some aspects of a pretty exciting and sometimes delightful life. They called me, among other things, a damned liar. But nobody from CASU-10 ever made such charges, because they knew better. They knew I had tracked down their jungle hideout at Madame Gardel's.

The book, from which the play and motion picture SOUTH PACIFIC were taken, was born one night at the CASU-10 hideaway. A Navy nurse, whose name I never knew, was married to an Army pilot, whose name I have forgotten. To celebrate the nuptials, we had assembled a pretty substantial wedding feast; the best, in fact, that could be stolen from closely guarded naval stores. Madame Gardel had invited to her plantation an entire tribe of jungle dancers. French planters had brought in jeeploads of wine and cognac. And we killed about half a dozen steers for a barbecue. There, in the depths of the jungle, the wedding was performed by a military chaplain who alternately read from the Service and stared at the tons of government gear around him.

Nothing that I have ever written about the South Pacific could equal, in inventiveness, the facts that occurred there, and I have often wished that self-appointed critics, who dismiss my report of the Pacific as 'made-up romancing,' could have seen that 'improbable' wedding.

In the evenings, while Jim and Garcia and Morrison made their tours of the island in my jeep and made their own discoveries --Garcia ferreted out Madame Gardel's, too, and muscled in on the joint--I sat in the long, drafty tin hut and typed out my recollections of what I had seen and heard. Next morning the touring trio would read what I had written and tear it apart.

With this division of labor we proceeded to fight our war. In time I suppose I came to know my island as well as any man could, and from this knowledge I tried to compose a report of what life was actually like on a Pacific backwater. The fighting part I had experienced earlier at the front; and my midnight notes became a fusion of these two aspects of war.

The book, when published, bore no dedication page. Today, if I were writing it, I would surely dedicate it to Jim and Garcia and Morrison, and to the Navy nurse whose wedding I attended. (I was invited because I had found a way to hijack nearly a half truckload of beer.)

My commander made captain, and his commander made admiral. Little Garcia won a commendation for one of the bravest acts I have every known a man to perform, and the Navy nurse and her pilot husband lived happily ever after ...I hope.

James A. Michener

--James A Michener

the deed .....

I

Before the curtain went up at the Majestic Theatre in New York on 7 April 1949, the original stage version of *SOUTH PACIFIC* was a success. For Richard Rodgers, composer, and Oscar Hammerstein II, librettist and lyric writer, had already demonstrated a genius for transmuting literary material into the warmth and wonder of musical theatre.

With the production of *Oklahoma!* in 1943 they had turned the stereotyped formula of the Broadway musical comedy into an art form that revolutionized the popular musical theatre. By taste, honesty and creative imagination they had made an organic work of lyrical art out of a familiar entertainment medium. Six years later, *SOUTH PACIFIC* was a work in their own tradition. Behind it were *Oklahoma!*, *Carousel* and *Allegro*—integrated musical plays in which music, story, dancing and decor expressed a single point of view. In the circumstances, no one doubted that *SOUTH PACIFIC* was going to be a piece of genuine stage literature.

In *SOUTH PACIFIC*, Nellie Forbush, Emile de Becque, Luther Billis, Lieutenant Cable, Liat and Bloody Mary are fabulous characters because James Michener, who wrote the original short stories, and Mr Rodgers and Mr Hammerstein, who wrote the musical drama, in association with Joshua Logan, have added their own dimensions. If they had been men of less artistic stature, Nellie Forbush might have been a chippie, Emile de Becque an opportunist and Lieutenant Cable a commonplace sensualist. But all these characters contain a measure of humility, sympathy and taste. They are decent people; they have the forbearance of people who respect the rights of others. They have conscience. For they are basically the children of the writers who have created them through the process of blending personal insight and personal ideals into the raw material of life.

(overleaf)

II

Mr Rodgers and Mr Hammerstein are New York theatre writers, each of whom had been born and reared in New York City, each of whom had had fifteen or twenty years of professional experience before they collaborated.

There was no tradition of the stage in Mr Rodgers' family. But both he and Mr Hammerstein fell in love with the theatre at early ages.

When Mr Rodgers was in his early teens he was particularly enraptured by the famous 'Princess musicals' by Guy Bolton, P G Wodehouse and Jerome Kern—small shows noted for their humor and melody. As a composer today, Mr Rodgers is in the tradition of Jerome Kern, whose musical roots were in Europe and whose heart was in America.

Although Mr Hammerstein's father and grandfather were in show business, his father (discouraged no doubt by the opera disasters of Oscar I) took a jaundiced view of the theatre and wanted his son to follow a respectable profession, like the law. But it was a futile hope, although Oscar II dutifully studied law to please his father and once even worked as an uninspired server of summonses.

Mr Rodgers was forty years of age and Mr Hammerstein forty-seven when their professional association began with *Oklahoma!*. But their lives had crossed at many places before. Although New York is a huge city, departmentalized into neighborhoods and business and cultural groups, it does not separate people who are interested in the same things. To immigrants from other parts of America, New York often seems like a secret society — a benign Mafia — in which native New Yorkers appear to be interrelated in some mysterious network of association, as if they had all grown up together intimately.

Now that Mr Rodgers and Mr Hammerstein have become partners in the most illustrious collaboration since Gilbert and Sullivan, hundreds of writers have searched the records and discovered facts that make the collaboration look preordained. For instance, Mr Rodgers and Mr Hammerstein grew up in the same neighborhood, attended the same summer camp and, at different times, became students at Columbia University. Mr Rodgers' older brother, Mortimer, was a fraternity brother of Mr Hammerstein at Columbia. Mr Rodgers and Mr Hammerstein were both involved in the Columbia annual musical shows. Mr Hammerstein was on the committee that accepted Mr Rodgers' score for a varsity show.

A year previously Mr Hammerstein had written the lyrics to two of Mr Rodgers' first songs—"Can It" and "Weakness"—in a boys' club show called *Up Stage and Down*. There were many other brief associations. But when Mr Rodgers and Mr Hammerstein started to work professionally in the theatre, they followed different paths.

III

Mr Rodgers' professional career began in 1920 with *Poor Little Ritz Girl*. The lyrics for his songs were written by the late Larry Hart, a brilliant, witty lyricist. That collaboration lasted for a long time. Together they wrote the music and lyrics for such memorable musical shows as *The Garrick Gaieties* (their first notable success), *Dearest Enemy, A Connecticut Yankee, Present Arms, Simple Simon, Jumbo, On Your Toes, Babes in Arms, I'd Rather Be Right, I Married an Angel, The Boys from Syracuse, Pal Joey* and *By Jupiter*. Among their songs were "My Heart Stood Still" and "With a Song in My Heart," which are part of the musical language of today.

Meanwhile, Mr Hammerstein was writing (or collaborating on) the books and lyrics of equally famous musicals like *Rose-Marie, The Desert Song, Sunny, Show Boat, Music in the Air, The New Moon, Very Warm for May* and *Carmen Jones*. His happiest collaborations were with Jerome Kern. They wrote "Ol' Man River," which has become part of the folklore of America.

In 1942, both Mr Rodgers and Mr Hammerstein had reached the ends of their respective roads. Larry Hart, an increasingly neurotic man, could no longer write the sharp, sophisticated lyrics expected of a Rodgers and Hart song. He died in 1943. Mr Hammerstein, who wrote lyrics and libretti in a more romantic style, had suffered a recent setback. It looked as though his career might be already finished.

The Theatre Guild was in a similar position. It had had a series of failures that were disastrous. Looking around for something that might restore the Guild's financial stability, its directors asked Mr Rodgers if he would be interested in writing a musical score for Lynn Riggs' romantic folk comedy, *Green Grow the Lilacs*, originally staged in 1931. Mr Rodgers liked the idea. Looking around for a suitable collaborator, he asked Mr Hammerstein. Since Mr Hammerstein had at one time tried to persuade Jerome Kern to make a musical out of the same script, he was happy to accept the assignment.

IV

The history of the musical theatre establishes one basic fact: memorable works are written only by composers and librettists whose

writing is of equal quality. Good scores have perished because the libretti were inferior, good libretti lost because the scores did not dramatize them well.

The collaboration of Mr Rodgers and Mr Hammerstein is one of the exceedingly rare good ones. It has released in each of them gifts and qualities that previously had been inadequately expressed. "What happened between Oscar and me was almost chemical," Mr Rodgers remarked to David Ewen, his biographer. "Put the right components together and an explosion takes place. Oscar and I hit it off from the day we began discussing the show [*Oklahoma!*]."

Part of the chemical reaction involved artistic integrity. They did not write *Oklahoma!* with the idea of changing the formula of musical comedy. They were solely concerned with finding the best way to convey the joyousness of the story. Had they followed the formula of musical comedy, they would have opened with a brassy chorus of farm girls and cowboys and with an explosive barrage from the orchestra. Instead, they began on a quieter note which the audience found fresh and exhilarating.

SOUTH PACIFIC also opens quietly. It begins with a tender song for two children, which is as guileless as a nursery tune. Mr Rodgers and Mr Hammerstein are both expert theatre technicians: they know how to introduce characters and develop stories in a way that seizes on and holds the imagination of the audience. But in the two instances discussed above, technique coincides with artistic integrity. It illuminates the text. It is not clever; it is honest.

When *Oklahoma!* (originally called *Away We Go*) was in the process of being produced, most Broadway showmen took a dim view of it. There was no such reluctance about *SOUTH PACIFIC*.

V

Mr Rodgers and Mr Hammerstein were thus in an enviable position as men of the theatre when they settled down to the writing of *SOUTH PACIFIC*. They could enjoy complete freedom from the sophistication of Broadway. Having established his reputation as a notable song writer, Mr Rodgers was now free to express a warmth, faith and sincerity that had never had a good outlet before. And Mr Hammerstein, in turn, had entered into a partnership in which his natural high-mindedness and faith in simple truths did not appear to be naive but carried weight, because they strengthened the themes and illuminated characters.

In the original plan, *SOUTH PA-CIFIC* was to be a dramatization of the rueful romance between Lieutenant Cable and Liat, the sweet native girl. This was the tale in Mr Michener's collection of South Pacific stories that had seemed most suitable. But the more they thought about it, the more Mr Rodgers and Mr Hammerstein lost interest in it. It seemed to them too much like the familiar theme of *Madame Butterfly*. Their enthusiasm for the project was revived when they considered another tale in Mr Michener's book: the tale of the American nurse and the French planter. They accordingly made Nellie and Emile the chief characters, and Lieutenant Cable and Liat the characters in a second theme, which would complement and develop the main story.

Both of these themes involve the subject of racial tolerance—not a subject that most theatre writers would exploit for popular entertainment. It is specifically stated in "You've Got To Be Taught," the slightly bitter, reflective melody that Lieutenant Cable sings.

But many people do not realize that the main theme of *SOUTH PACIFIC* also involves racial tolerance. Nellie Forbush, the hick from Little Rock, as she calls herself, is shocked when she discovers that Emile de Becque is the father of the flower-like, half-caste children who open the play. It takes the impact of a world war and her experiences on the island to shake the provinciality out of her character.

Since the authors of *SOUTH PA-CIFIC* are artists, they do not write propaganda. Propaganda manipulates the truth to prove a point. But art that has real validity is composed of moral principle as well as nature, the principle being the contribution of civilized people. *SOUTH PACIFIC* is extraordinary entertainment. In addition to the beauty of the music and lyrics and the portraits of character, it has humor, gusto, irony, horseplay and conviviality.

There is nothing in *SOUTH PA-CIFIC* that a pair of hacks could not translate into a brassy, whirlwind song-and-dance show with smart jokes and bawdy fooling. But the modesty of Emile, the good-heartedness of Nellie, the conscience of Lieutenant Cable, the grace of Liat, the heartiness of Bloody Mary and the comic brashness of Billis constitute a world of hospitality, beauty, ethics and goodwill that reflects the characters of the authors. It is fortunate for all of us that, by force of circumstances, Mr Rodgers and Mr Hammerstein came together at a period in their lives when they could bring each other professional experience and maturity of thought.

—Brooks Atkinson
Drama Critic,
The New York Times

in song and

SOUTH PACIFIC

A Musical Play appears on a theatre marquee and immediately conjures up visions of waving palm trees, lapping waters and seductive, brown-skinned maidens undulating in the soft evening breeze.

As an individual I certainly have nothing against palm trees and I am willing to declare myself in favor of brown-skinned maidens any time, but I would deeply loathe the task of composing the sort of music commonly associated with this atmosphere. It consists, traditionally, of what Oscar Hammerstein refers to as 'sleepy lagoon' strains. To be technical, these strains are usually written in four-quarter time and in intervals of major thirds employed consecutively. The practical result, for me at least, is an impaired complexion, due to excessive sweetness, and an irresistible lethargy.

In approaching the problem of supplying an original score for SOUTH PACIFIC, I knew I had to employ a musical approach that would enliven the scene rather than enervate it. The solution came from the two main characters themselves. Emile de Becque, a 'cultured Frenchman,' could sing phrases that were fairly sophisticated and carried the echoes of his continental upbringing: "This Nearly Was Mine," "Some Enchanted Evening." Nellie Forbush, on the other hand, and in happy contrast, could sing about her "Wonderful Guy" and proclaim with an American voice, "I'm Gonna Wash That Man Right Outa My Hair." The nurses and all the members of the armed forces were automatically confined to the American idiom so that only Bloody Mary and Liat required tunes that sang with a tropical island inflection. These songs lent a nice change of pace and a graceful contrast to the American- and European-sounding melodies. The little song done by the two native children took the form of a nursery piece, obviously taught them by their French father. This made possible still another change of tempo and musical color. Actually, I have been asked many times whether or not "Dites Moi" was an old French nursery song. I find the question highly flattering. It was not. I wrote it.

Once again the dramatic content of SOUTH PACIFIC allowed me to roam musically, this time into the field of burlesque. "Honey Bun" and all the musical material in the show put on by the 'service' girls and boys had to be the sort that would afford entertainment and fun for a 'service' audience as well as the commercial audience coming to see SOUTH PACIFIC. Apparently it did just that, but no one had more fun and entertainment than I did in writing the music for SOUTH PACIFIC.

—Richard Rodgers

story . . . . .

In the early thirties, when the theatre became a dubious specu-
lation for a man with a sizeable family, I deserted it for the more secure life of
a Hollywood playwright. After a year or so of screen 'conditioning' I took my
wife one evening to a play in Los Angeles. It contained two of our favorite
Broadway stars. After the curtain rose we were both shocked by the strange
performances we were witnessing. The two stars and the entire company
seemed to be shouting. They were not really shouting, of course; they were
'projecting.' They were reading their lines with natural inflections but adding
that little extra push that would carry the words all the way up to the last row
in the second balcony. Our difficulties in the beginning of the first act proved
that my wife and I had become used to screen acting.

I have been asked by many people—and I expect to be asked
by many more —"How does the screen cast of 'South Pacific' compare with the
stage cast?" My answer is that you can make no direct comparison. Magnificent
as was the performance on the stage, had it been photographed it would have
looked like over-acting and over-singing. How could it be otherwise? If you
play against painted scenery, within the framework of a proscenium and behind
a filled orchestra pit, how could you possibly give the same performance that
would be required in real tropical foliage on a real island, with a microphone
just above and a camera a few feet away?

Stage acting is not better than screen acting, nor is screen acting better than stage acting. They are different, that's all. So when I am asked
to compare the two casts, I truthfully say that each within its own medium is
equally satisfying and exciting to me as an author. I thought the stage cast as
perfect as a cast could be. In the same way, I don't believe I have ever seen the
story of a musical picture acted with the sincerity and emotional honesty that
I find in *SOUTH PACIFIC*. Nor have songs been introduced and performed
with as much grace and regard to story value.

Songs have always been a problem in musical pictures. Story
and music seemed like separate things. In *SOUTH PACIFIC* the device of
changing the light and texture of the pictures for a musical number is a very
important contribution. It is a kind of subtle acknowledgment that the literal
reality of dialogue will be suspended for a moment while we pretend that
people express their thoughts and feelings in song. It helps our imagination
to find the poetry that sings inside us at certain times but which our fumbling
prose does not express.

—Oscar Hammerstein II

the studio......

"Damn the solar system; bad light, planets too distant, pestered with comets; feeble contrivance; could make a better one myself," wrote Francis Lord Jeffrey, famous essayist and jurist of the last century.

His lordship should have been a motion picture producer. He had the right qualifications: a healthy reluctance to accept even the highest order of things as they are; a determination to make them bigger, better and brighter; the self-confidence to believe that he could bring it off.

Now I, a producer, have no ambitions concerning the solar system. But I *have* undertaken its theatrical equivalent: to produce a motion picture version of Rodgers and Hammerstein's *SOUTH PACIFIC*.

The original play was a big, big show, buoyant with unforgettable music; colorful, boisterous, tragic, tender and romantic—one of the immortal classics of the stage.

Yet we felt that the filmed *SOUTH PACIFIC* had to be something more than a literal translation. It had to offer something new to the 25 million people who have crowded theatres all over the world to see it these past nine years. New . . . to take advantage of the vast panoramic screen and the beauty and color of authentic backgrounds; new . . . to include the exciting physical action that could only be mentioned on the stage; new . . . to give the show's original creators: Rodgers, Hammerstein and Logan, a chance to do more than merely repeat, a chance to express themselves afresh in the fresh idiom of the screen.

It was a gamble, of course. We are so often asked: "What does a producer *do*, anyway?" The answer is simply: "He gambles." He gambles money, time, talent, his own reputation, even his job, on the chance that he can improve something by properly adapting and enlarging it. And, like all successful gamblers, he doesn't count his chips when he thinks he holds a winning hand. (We fail only when we 'play it safe,' when we scale down and, in that way, belittle our material.)

So we took *SOUTH PACIFIC* from the traditional confines of the stage and threw it into all outdoors. To film Michener's story we went to Michener's world. Six months before shooting with the principals began, we flew a production company to the Fiji Islands, where they spent four weeks photographing backgrounds (scenic and human) in fantastic color and capturing for the large Todd-AO screen the magic of love-haunted Bali Ha'i.

For our major location, we chose an island often called the most beautiful in the world: Kauai. There we sent our cast and a production company comprising a hundred and seventy-eight men and women, the finest artists and technicians available at Twentieth Century-Fox. They took four shiploads of material: cameras, lights, grip equipment, costumes, rolling stock, construction material and properties. They built thousands of square feet of concrete road, docks and loading aprons. They spent days 'exterior decorating'— and days more returning the landscape to its original form. They ate a total of seventy-five thousand meals.

We shot on Kauai for nine weeks, exposing two hundred thousand feet of Todd-AO film, including extensive coverage of a combined Naval and Marine operation—the largest task force ever photographed for use in a commercial film.

At the home studio, we shot on four of our huge sound stages. Then the entire production was turned over to the editors, the sound cutters, the recording mixers, the laboratory technicians, and later to Alfred Newman's hundred and twenty five piece orchestra for final recording.

I have quoted figures freely because I want to give you some idea of the scale of the operation. Was it extravagant? We don't think so. We think we were only doing justice to a great property.

And what is the end product, the final result of all this planning and spending, this racking of brains, this flying over oceans, loading and unloading of equipment, waiting for the right light and straining for the exact effect, the infinitesimally correct gesture of a hand or intonation of a voice?

A cynic might say that we have finally achieved a strip of colored celluloid, seventy millimeters wide and four miles long, with pictures down its center and sounds imprisoned in magnetic patterns on its sides.

But we hope that what we have created will add up to a great deal more. We hope we have succeeded in capturing the magic of *SOUTH PACIFIC* as only the Todd-AO camera could have captured it. We hope that we have provided the way to some enchanted evenings in a world bigger, better and brighter than life.

—Buddy Adler

the continuity . . . . .

O.K.

Buddy Adler

Have only out-takes of these right now.
Sent rough cut to Archer for title make up.

Bob Simpson

Note: Film Editor

TITLES OVER FILM SHOT IN FIJI, ESPIRITU, ETC-
RAY KELLOGG'S UNIT—SHOWING SOUTH PACIFIC:
VARIOUS LOCATIONS, CONDITIONS. LAST TITLE
FADES ON SOLITARY PBY IN CLEAR BLUE SKY

SC7 PBY COCKPIT - DAY - CABLE AND ADAMS —
(DIALOG ABOUT PLANTER EMILE DE BECQUE)

Yellow + 85 filter Carl

Note: An '85' is a
blue-absorption
filter

A Cockeyed Optimist . . .

SC17 DE BECQUE'S TERRACE - CAMERA ON NELLIE
EMILE IN F.G.

The Soliloquy

SC19   LONG SHOT - CUT TO: CLOSEUP OF NELLIE
(HER VOICE OVER)

SC19A   CLOSE SHOT - CAM. PULLS BACK, HOLDS AS THEY WALK O.S.

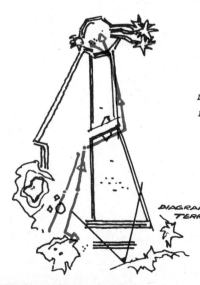

Dites-Moi
Pourquoi . . .

DIAGRAM
TERRACE

SC21   FULL SHOT - NGANA AND JEROME, EMILE

SC 22   BLOODY MARY'S BEACH   – LOW SHOT ON PROF. AND MEN

Cut straight to this after we are in from high boom — Sudden change — adds to feeling of fun & excitement —

Josh Logan

SC 23   MED. SHOT – CAM. ON BILLIS AND MARY

SC 25   LOWER BEACH –   LONG SHOT
INSERT : LAUNDRY

Insert & items unnecessary

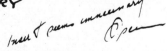

THERE   IS   NOTHING   LIKE   A   DAME ! ! !

SC 26 A GROUP SHOT . ANGLE - QUICK CUT TO FRONT ON MUSIC CUE

See Score. (vocal cue is "gusty, womanly female, feminine dame".) RR

Note: See pp 6-10

Note: See pp 34-37

Bay Island as Third Character!

SC 28 - END OF PIER.- M.S.- CABLE AND MARY
(DIALOG: "YOU VERY SAXY MAN!")

Bali Ha'i . . .

:29 CLOSE SHOT - CAM. PANS RT TO:

SC 29 A BALI HA'i - CABLE'S P.O.V.

SC 37 HQ. (BRACKETT'S OFFICE) - CABLE,
BRACKETT, HARBISON, NELLIE

what's the time on this sequence
now? That one cut is what it
needed.   DR

I'M GONNA

WASH THAT MAN

RIGHT OUTA MY HAIR! ...

SC 39 - NURSES' BEACH -
DOWN SHOT ON GROUP

3-Shot?! That horse was the biggest
ham ever! Ben Kadish

Note: Asst
Director

SC 42 THREE SHOT -
NELLIE UNDER TOWEL

(Did you killed Amber take RED?)

*Amber +85 + diffused edge.
R C*

SC 45 EDGE OF NURSES BEACH - MED SHOT

I'M IN LOVE WITH A WONDERFUL GUY . . .

SC 51 SHORE LINE - WIDE ANGLE LONG SHOT - (BUG EYE LENS)

*Love this sequence
O.P.*

SC 59 H.Q - M.C.S - CUT TO

SC 59A CAM PANS HIS EXIT

*Al. Ken —
our Island is in
great voice
today —!*

BALI HA'I (singing)

SC 65 BALI HA'i BEACH-DAY- BOOM SHOT — CAM SWINGS IN LT.,
PANS RT. TO APPROACHING BOAT.

*We're using the boom footage for our
master shot — this for undercuts only —
Josh*

SC 66 PIER — BOAT'S ARRIVAL
LONG SHOT

SC 68 - CAM TRUCKS BACK AS BILLIS, CABLE PASS NATIVE GIRLS

SC 71 VILLAGE - MARY - (DIALOG:
"YOU COME WITH ME, LOOTELLAN")

SC 78A (INTERCUT) JUNGLE PATH-
LIAT

SC 78 TROPICAL GARDEN -
UP SHOT ON CABLE, MARY

SC 82 BAMBOO BRIDGE -
HIGH LONG SHOT

Stage 8: "Sultan" set, lit with yellow ss rep.
(Smoke for mist effect - Spec Effect Dept. (Schott)
F. Hall

#59 Amber Gels
Yellow Carbon
28, 100 amps
Bob Henderson

Note: Fred is the 'Gaffer,'
i e, Head of the Lighting crew;
Bob is his 'Best Boy,' i e, Assistant

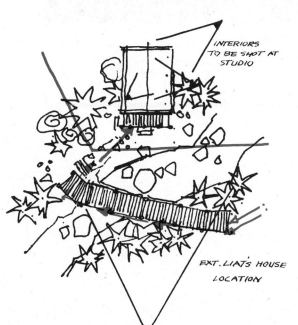

INTERIORS
TO BE SHOT AT
STUDIO

EXT. LIAT'S HOUSE
LOCATION

SC 90 LIAT'S HOUSE - CLOSE UP.

SC91 A FULL SHOT
THE CHIEF

SC91 KRAAL - SUNDOWN -
BOAR'S TOOTH CEREMONY

SC91 B LONG SHOT - CAM. MOVES IN SLOWLY TO FIRE PIT.

SC91C HIGH SHOT "FLOWERGIRLS"
MEDICINE MAN IN F.G.

Note: The BTC is based primarily on a Malekula tribal dance but 12 other tribes and 48 source references were used by LeRoy Prinz to create the choreography

Younger than springtime . . .

Really fine orchestration.
DR

SC94 LIAT'S HOUSE -TWILIGHT. LOW SHOT

SC95 BAMBOO BRIDGE. UP SHOT- CAM. TRUCKS WITH CABLE ON EXIT

Magenta no so't cousin's
not for much. Carol

Note: See pp 40-41

SC 96 BALI HA'i BEACH
NIGHT- BOOM SHOT

COSTUME DESIGN - D.J. -
NELLIE - CHANGE 5
SC 101 - 106 -

SC 102 TERRACE - NIGHT - EXTR.
LONG SHOT

Green better met of
L1.

SC 104

Some Enchanted Evening . . .

Oscar, Dick — I'd like to screen this
first thing in the morning —

Josh

Ken wants us to learn this tape.
RR

Note: Ken is
Ken Darby,
Vocal Coach

EMILE (mimicking Nellic)
Note: See Scenes 39-42

SC 103   FULL SHOT
EMILE UNDER CAPE

Let's keep our distance here
Oscar

SC 106 TWO SHOT — CUT TO: CLOSE UP OF
NELLIE-TEARS -

COSTUME DESIGN - OJ - LIAT -
CHANGE 2 - SC 114-118

SC 114 WATERFALL -DAY- EXTR.
LONG SHOT

Yellowtop + smoke in set
for magical- mistaires quality X
This should have a kind of Rousseau
feeling - (Paul)

SC 116

Happy -- Happy Talk . . .

Dick likes new
arrangement of intro -
Recording tomorrow
Al Newman

Note : See pp 38-39

SC 115 FULL SHOT - TRIO AT EDGE
OF POOL

And this a Gauguin!   Josh

SC 118 THREE SHOT - CUT TO: CLOSE UP OF
HAT - TEARS

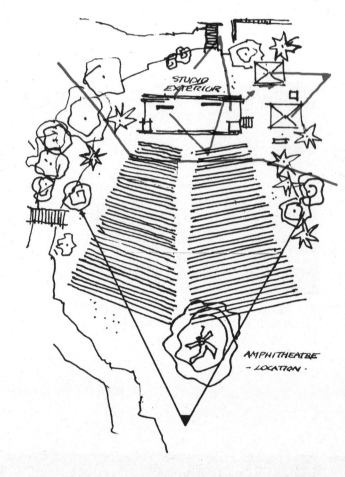

AMPHITHEATRE
- LOCATION -

HONEY BUN . . .

SC 126 AMPHITHEATRE - NELLIE AND BILLIS

SC 126A REVERSE SHOT - AUDIENCE'S P.O.V

SC 126B (INTERCUT) CLOSER
ON NELLIE

SC 126 C (INTERCUT) SC 126 B
CONTINUED

See Score. (come cut
orchestration as is!)
DR

Relate 2nd chorus
Nellie's volume too high for Cable's
Make just audible, almost a hum
Open

Note: See
pp 6-11

My Girl Back Home . . .

SC 127 BACKSTAGE
(CLOSE SHOT (EMILE'S VOICE OVER)

SC 129 STAGE (PLANE PLATFORM) TWO SHOT

You've Got To Be Taught . . .

SC 130 BACKSTAGE - ON CABLE

Majority Backstage stuff shot
with process plates no 85 RodHant

This Nearly Was Mine . . .

SC 131 BACKSTAGE - ON EMILE

ESTIMATED MUSIC BUDGET
MINUTES OF MUSIC:

Note: Studio Manager

SC137 PBY COMPARTMENT - DAY -
EMILE, BILLIS, CABLE, ADAMS

(LEON for 133 B- EXTERIOR - R.B. & R.3 officers-
...what info do you want- off 6 A.M.
test take 216 ? RED)

NAVY FIGHTERS

ZERO

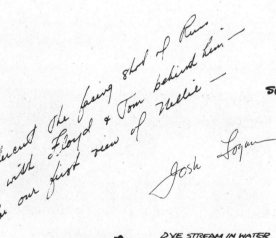

DYE STREAM IN WATER

BILLIS IN RUBBER RAFT

Intercut the facing shot of Rum
— with Floyd & Tom behind him —
for our first view of Nellie —

Josh Logan

SC 183 CAVE ON ENEMY ISLAND -
TILT SHOT

SC 197 HOSPITAL - PILOT IN BG. <u>IN FOCUS</u>
(DIALOG ABOUT " THE FRENCHMAN ")

SC 205 HQ (RADIO ROOM) QUICK CUT TO
NELLIE'S ENTRANCE, REACTION

Render further +85 = complement into white area — Brando

SC 206   A LONELY PLACE - SUNSET - L.S.
MARY, LIAT, NELLIE.

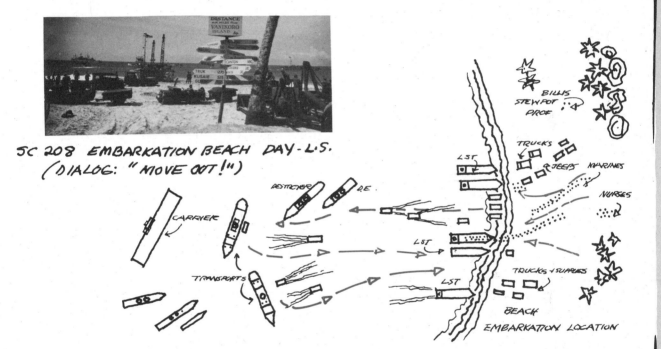

SC 208 EMBARKATION BEACH DAY - L.S.
(DIALOG: " MOVE OUT !")

BILLIS
STEW POT
PROF.

TRUCKS

JEEPS MARINES

NURSES

LST

DESTROYER   D.E.

CARRIER

TRANSPORTS

LST

LST

TRUCKS + SUPPLIES

BEACH
EMBARKATION LOCATION

Note: See pp 12-13

Final Cut.
Feb 10,
Buddy Adler

Dites-Moi
Pourquoi . . .

SC 233 TERRACE - DAY - NELLIE, NGANA, JEROME

For pe 235 use split from to f.g. from long shot   Osborn

the cast .....

Emile de Becque . . . . *Rossano Brazzi*

Nellie Forbush . . . . *Mitzi Gaynor*

Lt Joseph Cable . . . . *John Kerr*

t h e   p e r f e c t   s h o w

Luther Billis . . . . Ray Walston

Bloody Mary . . . . Juanita Hall

Liat . . . . France Nuyen

Capt Brackett . . . . Russ Brown

Professor . . . . Jack Mullaney

Stewpot . . . . Ken Clark

Comdr Harbison . . . . Floyd Simmons

Ngana, Emile's daughter . . . . Candace Lee

Jerome, Emile's son . . . . Warren Hsieh

Lt Adams . . . . Tom Laughlin

i n

i n   t o d d - a o !

the direction ....

In recent years so much has been written about Joshua Logan and his many successes that it seems repetitious to add anything more on that score. In 1937, however, he had not yet directed a Broadway play. It was my good fortune that the first play he did direct was one of mine, *On Borrowed Time*. And it was something he said to me at our first meeting that I feel indicated the way he was to go.

A luncheon had been arranged by the producer so that Josh and I could meet and the three of us discuss the play. It had been decided to lunch later than the regular luncheon hour to have the place to ourselves. We did. In fact, when I arrived there was no one there at all—except one self-absorbed young man sitting over in a corner. I waited for some time and had just begun to realize that either I had the place and time wrong or something must have happened to prevent Josh and the producer from coming when the man over in the corner rose and came to my table.

"Are you Paul Osborn?" he asked.

I said I was.

"My name's Josh Logan." After a polite interval of preliminaries, he said: "I'm crazy about the play, but I think it goes all wrong at the end. In fact, I don't think there *is* an end."

"I'm afraid you're right," I agreed. "But what can I do about it?"

"We've got to get in and dig and find out what's wrong," he answered. "It would be ridiculous to put this play on until we get it right."

So we started to dig and by the time the producer arrived to introduce us we had done quite a lot of digging. We've more or less been digging ever since.

Josh Logan is now acknowledged to be one of our finest directors. He brings to the theatre excitement and color and originality. Now, that's all well and good. It is wonderful to see fine actors giving their best performances; it is wonderful to see on the screen 'pictures' that have not been seen before—and yet Josh Logan's genius as a director lies, to my way of thinking, much deeper than that.

It lies in the statement he, the director, made to me that first day at lunch, long before any actor or set was thought of: "We've got to dig into this play and find out what's wrong with it."

It lies in his primary concern with getting— as Aristotle says in his *Poetics*—"the Plot so framed that, even without seeing the things that take place, he who simply hears the account of them shall be filled with horror and pity at the incidents."

It lies in the kind of painstaking, arduous, behind-the-scenes 'digging' that Josh puts into a script before he even thinks of doing it.

—Paul Osborn

Although the screen version of SOUTH PACIFIC may seem to, and indeed does, differ in almost every scene from the original play, the two are basically the same. As an example, "Happy Talk" in the film is played during the daylight hours in and about a tropical pool, whereas on the stage it took place at night in the bushes near the amphitheatre where the Thanksgiving show was in progress. Essentially, however, they are both the same versions of this famous song: an old Tonkinese woman and her daughter are elaborating on the joys of 'lotus eating' to a young Philadelphian.

Paul Osborn, one of America's distinguished playwrights, has, in preparing the screenplay, taken our original stage version and rewritten episodes so that we could take advantage of their most visually exciting settings. He has put in dramatic form scenes that on the stage could only be talked about. But Osborn has said that he was too fond of the original to do anything drastic that would disturb its basic humors, moods and even continuity.

What, then, is the difference between the two? Is the screen version simply an 'opened up' recapitulation of the play? 'Opened up' is a Hollywood expression, very handy for describing the way a movie can show vast crowds, aerial combat, an entire naval task force at sea and various other spectacular pleasures in the very same story, where on the stage these exciting moments could only be described in dialogue.

The difference between a motion picture and stage version of the same story is a very personal thing. It is my feeling that a member of the legitimate theatre audience experiences what almost amounts to physical contact with the actor. Both he and the actor are in the same room. They can hear each other, one when he speaks, the other when he laughs or applauds. In both there is a sense of taking part in an event while it is actually occurring. Subconsciously, in successful theatre, the man in the audience feels he is helping the story along by showing his approval of the actor or by giving him his rapt attention. The actor hears or feels this approval and is often encouraged to give a more creative performance. It is a reciprocal thing, a kind of long-distance love affair. Sometimes this is referred to as 'audience participation.'

An obvious example of this, on the stage, was Nellie's performance of "Honey Bun" in the Thanksgiving show. She sang directly to the audience and the audience was supposed to pretend it was a mass of GIs looking at an amateur show far off in the South Pacific. Men on the side of the stage spilling down into the audience indicated the attitude that the real audience was supposed to take. The audience took up its role immediately and enthusiastically. It was a real case of the audience and the actors both being in the show. Yet, through the tremendous sense of participation made possible by Todd-AO, we were able to achieve the same effect.

The film provides another, stronger and more important link with its audience: the close-up. With the Todd-AO lens, we in the audience can get so close to Nellie's face that we see behind her facade. We can tell by the color of her skin, by her breathing, that she is only pretending to be exuberant. We are close enough to read in her eyes the anguish she carries because of her break with Emile de Becque.

Also, we participate with the actors on film because we can move with them. The trip to Bali Ha'i, for instance, is a trip in actual fact rather than something suggested by a few props, a few lines of dialogue and some sketchy lighting. We are in the boat with Billis and Cable; we walk along the beach with them, peeking at the girls. We can also tag along on Cable's delirious visits with Liat; we can swim with them, slide with them down the waterfall, run close to their heels through the woods. We can even move right through the middle of the Boar's Tooth Ceremony, almost mingling with the primitive dancers. Later, we feel ourselves falling with Billis after he is discovered on the secret mission. We are in almost as much danger as de Becque and Cable while they are furtively transmitting information from the enemy-held island. And finally, we ourselves take part in the great mass movement of Operation Alligator as the task forces assemble on the South Pacific beaches for the first big push against the enemy. Surely this is audience participation that the stage could never achieve.

.   .   .

Each audience demands its own form of entertainment. . . . The reader of a book enjoys seeing with the back of his mind while his eyes are reading words. A playgoer accepts without question the fact that the ocean is painted and that thousands of men along a beach are just beyond the proscenium arch and therefore must be imagined rather than viewed. A filmgoer, seeing a man's eyes directed off-screen, demands a cut and another piece of film which shows what that man is looking at.

Because of these unconscious audience demands, each of the three versions of *SOUTH PACIFIC* was more elaborate than the one preceding.

Whereas Michener could sit at his typewriter and write his descriptions of the tropical seas, on the stage we had to paint scenery, rig lights and costume actors at a great deal of expense and inventiveness to achieve the same effect. For the screen we had to go even further: we had to move huge cameras, trucks and gargantuan generators, not to mention our army of actors and technicians, across oceans to the islands of Fiji and Samoa, and particularly to the island of Kauai.

.   .   .

One of the problems in transplanting a musical play to the screen is the treatment of its songs. The screen is a realistic medium. The camera records real sunlight, real wind, real sunburn and real sweat. When motion picture actors are seen in the middle of a desert, for instance, or far out at sea, and yet suddenly they break into song—accompanied by fifty violins—it often comes as a bit of a shock to the audience. "Where is that orchestra hidden—behind a sand dune, or in a passing plane?" is the reaction.

On the stage this has been no problem, since when the theatregoer is ushered to his seat he sees the orchestra tuning up, later on he sees the leader waving his baton when the overture is played, and during the performance he is always conscious of the musicians with the bottom vision of his eyes while the song is being sung. He is constantly reminded that he is in a theatre and that when the actor leaves off speaking and starts to sing it is simply a stylized way of playing the scene. It is not an intellectual step he makes but an emotional and subconscious one.

On the stage we help emphasize to the audience that a song is an extension of play-reality by dimming the lights and often by changing the spotlights from incandescent to arc. In this way we intensify the scene not only audibly but visually. And at the same time we force the audience's attention to the actor's face; it is in a sense a way of suggesting a close-up though the spectator may be sitting at the rear of the orchestra or in the balcony.

The legitimate theatregoer accepts this extension of mood without question. In making the screen version of *SOUTH PACIFIC* we felt that the motion picture audience would also accept it if we could devise the same sort of visual change. But the effect was not so easy to achieve on the screen, mostly because so many of our scenes were filmed out of doors —and the sun does not dim on cue.

Leon Shamroy made some bold experiments and succeeded in developing an ideal technique. He actually changed the color of the film as the songs started, by the use of various lights and filters. And to concentrate attention on the singer's face, he devised a system of blurring the edges of the screen, allowing our eyes to focus only on what was important. . . .   True, it was a case of the camera borrowing an effect from the stage. But this was only fair and right because, way back in 1949, when Jo Mielziner and I were planning the scenic effects for the original *SOUTH PACIFIC*, we worked out a system for moving from one scene upstage to another scene on the forestage by bringing the lights up on the first scene before we had dimmed them out on the other. For fractions of a second, two scenes were being played at the same time. It was an effect borrowed from the screen, known as the lap-dissolve.

If one were to argue all night I doubt if the question could be settled as to which version of a story is most difficult to achieve: book, play or picture. The original conception surely must have come out of all kinds of turmoil and hard-learned experience on Michener's part. Rodgers and Hammerstein and I can vouch for the fact that telling a story in dialogue and song on the stage is an extremely exacting task, the limits are so strict. Yet, oddly, because there are almost no limits, making a picture as big as *SOUTH PACIFIC* is just as demanding. Its creators have to learn how to take advantage of all that freedom. Which means they have to learn about all the arts, crafts, and technical sciences a motion picture studio has to offer.

Though, as the director, I had to be well-versed in certain of these elements, there were many I could thankfully ignore. They were the problems of the producer: that gifted and overburdened gentleman, Buddy Adler. It was he who set the production, who selected and arranged for the best talent to be found for each phase of film-making.

The book and the musical play told essentially the same story and so, I believe, does the picture. But, till now, only the music could be universally understood. Now, all of *SOUTH PACIFIC* will be able to be seen and enjoyed not only in America, Britain and Canada but also in Denmark, Egypt, France, Germany, Hawaii, Italy and Japan . . . everywhere, in fact, where people can go to a theatre for the fun of it.

—Joshua Logan

the score.....

So you think you know the score? Well, that's what I thought, too. It's easy, I told myself. All you have to do is take a nice, successful Broadway show like *SOUTH PACIFIC*, throw in a little extra music among the tropical foliage, blend well, color to taste, and presto! a gen-u-ine musical picture.

Then I found out what really happens on a Hollywood recording stage. First of all I had to get two things straight in my mind: the difference between the *score* and *scoring* for—shall we say? (yes, let's!)—*SOUTH PACIFIC*.

Now, the score is the original musical composition written by Richard Rodgers, without which . . .! Well, since the LP record album from the play is still, after nine years, one of the ten best-sellers in the country, who needs me to tell them how great Mr Rodgers' music is? Everybody seems to know it already! So, back to the score. Orchestrated for the stage by Richard Russell Bennett, it consists of an overture, thirteen songs, a dance, one reprise, and two end-of-act finales. So far so good. That was what was needed to put *SOUTH PACIFIC* on the stage.

But scoring the film version of *SOUTH PACIFIC* is another kettledrum of fish. It consists of the material I've just mentioned, with the addition of (1) two more songs by Rodgers and Hammerstein, (2) I don't know how many more reprises, (3) a huge ceremonial dance by Newman and Darby, and (4) all background music, including "Newman's Variation on a Theme by Rodgers" for Cable's walk through Bali Ha'i. All scoring for the film was done by Music Director Al Newman, his associate Ken Darby (". . . wherever voices were concerned"), and his orchestrators Ed Powell, Pete

King, and Bernard Mayers. I kept hearing about what an enormously complex business it all was. Yet, for the life of me, I couldn't see why.

They soon told me why. "Most musical pictures contain from 15 to 25 numbers: songs, dances, and reprises," they told me, "but Rodgers and Hammerstein's *SOUTH PACIFIC* has over fifty separate musical entities." (Whatever that means.) Most musical pictures pre-record one or two songs, record the rest while the film is being shot, and post-record all background music. When the *SOUTH PACIFIC* company left for Kauai, they took with them pre-recordings of *all* the songs and over an hour of background music because "the entire picture, excepting a few interiors shot at the studio, was shot on location across the Pacific," they told me. And because "it was Mr Logan's desire to use the background music as an impetus for many of the scenes."

Remember the scene where Nellie and Emile are dancing on the terrace? All the music for it was pre-recorded in Hollywood. Which meant that Al Newman and company had to plot, arrange, orchestrate, and record the music for a whole sequence before the sequence had been shot. It meant they had to anticipate what the director and cinematographer would do on actual location. It meant they even had to allow for bad weather! (And Kauai is notoriously wet.) It meant, in short, a wow of a headache.

But the real super-colossal headache came when all the post-scoring and post-recording had to be done. The edited picture was shown over and over and over and over. Then it was broken down scene by scene and sometimes even shot by shot. "It's at that point," Al Newman told me, "that the composer or adapter sits down with a blank

piece of manuscript paper and begins to worry like hell." Every scene was timed to the split second so that the music would conform to all the highs and lows of the dramatic action. When the manuscript—of "Newman's Variation on Another Theme by Rodgers"—was finished, the music orchestrated and rehearsed, recording began. A film marked with cue lines ('landmarks' and 'streamers') was projected before the conductor—Al Newman again—who wore headphones bringing him a tempo guide ('click track') from a previous recording. It was his job to bring all these elements together, somehow.

That describes a relatively simple bit of musical business. It only involved the conductor, a hundred and twenty-five piece orchestra, twelve or fifteen sound technicians, and someone (I think he's called a 'mixer') to figure out which part of the orchestra was to be picked up on which set of mikes. Todd-AO's hi-fi sound system has six channels—five for the speakers behind the screen, the sixth for all the auditorium speakers—and each channel has to be separately 'fed'. Now, straight background music, with no extensions or alterations, no vocals, no sound effects, no dialogue, goes on six tapes. If any other sound has to be heard at the same time, it is taken on a tape of its own. The day I met Bob Mayer, the music editor, he was working on a sequence that had, all together, twenty-nine separate tapes!

When the last bit of music had been recorded, all the sound—score, dialogue, etc—was edited, balanced, and finally 'striped' (photographed) onto a six-channel magnetic track.

As I was saying . . . all you need, to know the score, is a few hundred technicians, four or five musical geniuses, Richard Rodgers, and a great, big, wonderful Broadway show like *SOUTH PACIFIC*.

—S C Burchell

richard rodgers

alfred newman

ken darby

edward powell

pete king

bernard mayers

robert russell bennett

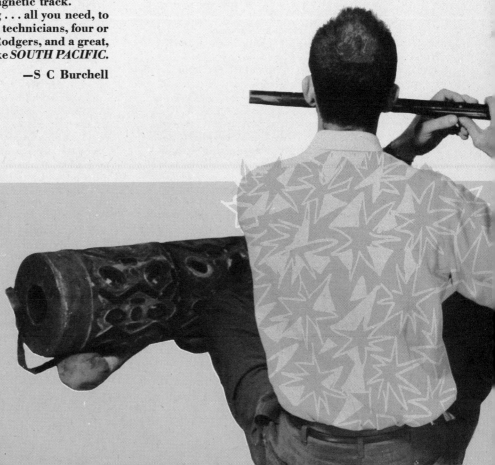

color + ...

Black: white; tall: short; shoe: foot; color: Shamroy. . . .

A Hollywood psychiatrist swears that every time he gives a Word Association Test to a motion picture executive, 'Shamroy' is the immediate response to the word 'color.' The reason? Leon Shamroy, A S C, is recognized as the finest color cinematographer in the world. But further, Leon Shamroy is and has a personality as brilliantly vivid as the films he makes.

Shamroy, Shammy, Leon— *never* Mister Shamroy—is taut, tanned, graying and irascible, given to conversing almost exclusively in expletives which visitors to the set claim range from Blush to Shocking Pink to Blue-in-the-face. During the filming of *SOUTH PACIFIC*, Shamroy took to wearing a bright red alpaca vest and/or startling straw headgear at the request of his crew who complained that, between the purple fog of his inevitable cigar and the mauve 'special effects' mist, they had difficulty locating him—particularly in his quieter moments.

Shamroy's motion picture career started unspectacularly in 1920 in the film lab of Fox Film Corporation. Between 1924 and 1927 he shot cliff-hangers and stunt pictures for Charles Hutchinson of Pathe. He filmed, and co-produced with Dr Paul Fejos, the experimental *Last Moment* (now, unfortunately, no longer extant), which was voted the Honor Film of 1928 by the National Board of Review. During 1928-29 he was associated with the pioneer of the documentary, Robert Flaherty. The next two years were spent photographing the Orient and Indonesia for the Huntington Ethnological Expedition—locales of his future *Love is a Many-Splendored Thing, The King and I* and *SOUTH PACIFIC*. Now a full-fledged cinematographer, in 1933 he went with B P Schulberg Productions, in '37 with Selznick International and in 1939 he returned to his first studio, *20th Century*-Fox Film Corporation, as Director of Photography. Since that time, Shamroy has won—at least once—every major honor awarded for cinematography.

Leon Shamroy differs from most motion picture cameramen in that he approaches a scene as a painter would do, viewing it through his mind's eye, while others tend toward a more naturalistic approach, taking the photographer's point of view. Cinematography and photography are two separate media. (Shamroy, who professes an inability to communicate without a camera, becomes quite eloquent on the subject). In photography, the individual shot is the goal. In cinematography, "individual shots can look great but when you put them together they spell nothing! A good shot is a shot that helps the picture from a dramatic standpoint. . . . When the audience gets hung up on the photography, it's no good. Maybe at the beginning of a sequence they might think, 'Isn't this a great shot'—all right—but then they have to get enveloped—involved in the story. . . . The little fickle things we did were for mood, for—to bring the audience into the picture. If it happened to be good photography too, fine, but . . . I'm not mortgaging my soul to photography!"

And perhaps he isn't. Yet Shamroy's work in *SOUTH PACIFIC* is pictorially as well as dramatically a work of art. According to Leo McCreary, his key grip on fifty-six pictures, Shamroy was the first cameraman to mix colored lights on a set. "I think he was even the first to use colored gelatins. He actually paints a scene like an artist does, a real artist—you know: Shamroy, the Old Master!—only he works with lights instead of paints to set the mood or composition, whatever effect he's trying to get."

Shamroy created a whole new color concept for *SOUTH PACIFIC*, based in part on an idea he had had in the back of his mind for years and in part on necessity. John de Cuir, the art director for the picture, accompanied him on a location survey. "Shammy was fit to be tied. Nothing was right. When the sun was out, he said it looked like a picture post card. When it was raining, which was most of the time—oh, and there'd just been a tidal wave— he'd get so mad we'd lose him completely." Shamroy phrases it differently. "When we were tramping around Kauai—we . . . near broke our necks on the debris—I said to Johnny, 'What the . . . are we doing here, for . . . sake? If I shoot *this*, it would look like a mourner's bench, like a . . . wake!' Everybody thinks of the South Seas as sparkling. It isn't. You get the sun here, and a rainbow here, and then it's gloomy over there. As we were walking through [the native village], I suddenly thought, 'I'd like to get something like Gauguin did with that magenta—,' and that's why I used a magenta filter actually. Then, near the waterfall, I thought of Rousseau—you know,

the French primitive painter—his detail, the green, the yellow seeping in. And also Covarrubias, those green ferns he had—And, over all, maybe some of the golden sunlight of Van Gogh. I shot 'Happy Talk' through a medium yellow filter—it was a dull, cloudy day, but it came out sunlight!"

Originally, Shamroy had planned to use his fabulous filters only for Bali Ha'i, the dream island. But when Logan and Hammerstein saw the color tests, a dream of their own was fulfilled. Finally musical interludes could stop being 'sore thumbs,' mere awkward conventions! So special filters were used for all the songs as well. Red Crawford, for thirty-five years Shamroy's right hand and alter ego (to be technical, his assistant cameraman), explains it. "When Lt Cable leaves Liat's house, he's walking on clouds, in a purple haze. So Leon put a magenta filter on the lens to symbolize his emotions. For 'Some Enchanted Evening,' he used a deep golden yellow, withdrawing it when Nellie snaps out of her golden daze on the line, 'Your jeep is waiting.' ... We used color filters throughout Bali Ha'i to give it a mystic, romantic feeling. Leon pioneered this in *The Egyptian*, in the embalming room sequence where he used green filters to give it an eerie look. So far as I know, that was the first time it was ever done."

As shooting picked up and the weather did not, the company had to depend more and more on Shamroy's ingenuity. Sunrise, day, late afternoon, sunset, dusk, twilight, night, all came out of his magic box of colors: rose-pale yellow, medium yellow, gold, amber, orange-magenta, magenta-blue, blue-green.

"I've made tough pictures, in the early days when we didn't have much money, but this—it's one of the biggest, but it's the toughest I ever worked on in my life! Not even to mention weather, the locations were tough—you couldn't reach them!, the equipment was tremendous ... yet, you know, there's nothing like adversity for success. You work five times as hard and it shows—not in a physical sense, but in a sort of spiritual sense. You don't get any of that run-of-the-mill nonsense."

Run-of-the-mill: Leon Shamroy? Never!

—Anne T Suivne

leon shamroy

the new TODD-AO .....

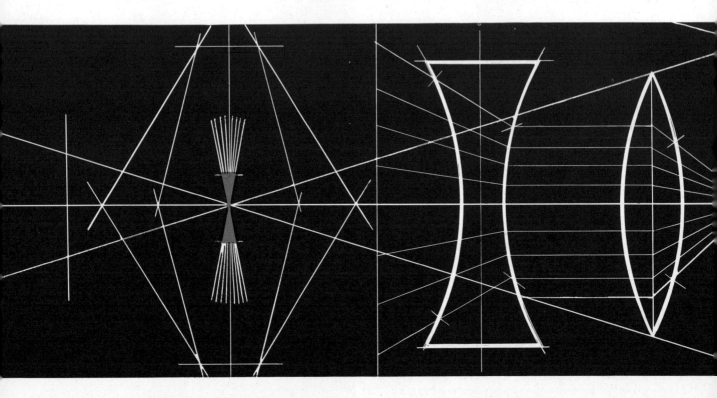

Todd-AO is the latest advance in an industry which many persist in describing, happily if somewhat inaccurately, as "in its infancy." The motion picture is an infant only in terms of its future; its lineage can be traced back to the late Middle Ages, when men first noticed the strange effect created by a *camera obscura*. A *camera obscura* was a small dark room with a peephole through which scenes from the sunlit world could be projected. There, on an ordinarily blank wall, the scenes were reproduced in miniature. Because the illusion of life was so strong and since "the image," according to Leonardo da Vinci, "is man's way to capture immortality," man had to wonder how the illusion could be made even more complete.

Today, Todd-AO, with its one hundred twenty-eight degrees of clear vision, has completed that illusion, wrapping its audience in images of utmost dramatic reality.

But behind the great explosion of light and color that is the modern film, we can detect the outlines of another drama, six centuries in the telling:

c 1344   First distinct mention of a *camera obscura* (but not made public until 1560)
     ' Leo Hebraeus ' (Levi ben Gerson)

c 1519   First practical demonstration of a *camera obscura*
First practical demonstration of a projector (with a plano-convex lens)
     Leonardo da Vinci

c 1568   First use of a convex lens on the *camera obscura* peephole, for clarity
     Daniel Barbaro

c 1822   First permanent photograph; a *camera obscura* had become a camera (a portable box)
     Joseph Niepce

1824   First formulation of the theory of persisting vision, an image-retaining peculiarity of the eye that makes motion pictures possible
     Peter Mark Roget (Roget's Thesaurus)

1837   First practical photographic process; the image was reproduced on a silvered metal plate
     Louis Daguerre and Isidor Niepce

1876   First mechanical system for reproducing recorded sound: the Phonograph
     Thomas Edison and William Dickson

1877   First motion study photographs (a race horse in action) taken by 24 cameras in sequence
     Eadweard Muybridge and John Isaacs

1887   First disc record
First lateral recording (the method used today)
     Emile Berliner

1888   First practical rollable film: gelatin emulsion-coated celluloid
     George Eastman

1889   First motion picture: the Kinetoscope, a battery-driven film strip moved through a camera by means of sprockets (coordinated with a phonograph, it was also the *first talking picture*)
     William Dickson, Edison's assistant

1894   First public showing of the Kinetoscope (without phonograph), a Peep Show
     Thomas Edison

1894   First portable hand-cranked motion picture camera
     Robert W Paul

1895   First public showing of the Cinématographe: a camera, developer, printer and *projector*-in-one
     Louis and Auguste Lumière

1898   First public showing of (synchronized) sound-on-cylinder talking pictures: minute-long scenes with famous theatrical personalities e g, Sarah Bernhardt, Coquelin
     French-made, based on Edison's Kinetoscope

1908   First mechanical color photographic system for motion pictures: Kinemacolor
     A G Smith and Charles Urban

c 1921   First experiments in sound-on-film; developed in Germany (the patents were bought by William Fox in 1927)
     Tri-Ergon

1923   First sound-on-film talking pictures: Phonofilm short subjects of vaudeville stars (abandoned when they failed to arouse sufficient interest)
     Lee De Forest

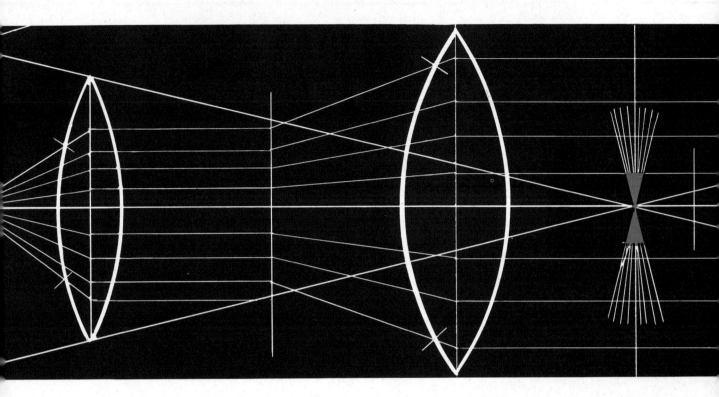

1923	First practical, economical color-reproduction system: Technicolor *Dr Herbert Kalmus*
1926	First sound-on-disc talking pictures: Vitaphone shorts of concert and vaudeville stars; also, a feature film with the first recorded sound effect (the slam of a door) and score: *Don Juan*, starring John Barrymore *Bell Telephone*
1926	First public showing of a three-projector, three-screen process (unnamed); a feature film: *Napoléon* *Abel Gance*
1927	First successful sound-on-film talking pictures: Fox Movietone newsreels (Movietone was the name of the sound system) *Theodore Case, ex-associate of De Forest*
1927	First sound-on disc (Vitaphone) feature film: *The Jazz Singer*, starring Al Jolson (three songs and a few lines of dialogue) *Bell Telephone*

By the end of 1928, sound-on-film à la Movietone proved preferable to sound-on-discs à la Vitaphone. In 1931, Western Electric and RCA took over production of a standardized sound-on-film system.

1928	First public showing of anamorphic lens experiments *Dr Henri Chrétien*
1929	First public showing of wide-screen experiments *Fox Films, Paramount Pictures*
1933	First public showing of stereoscopic (3-D) experiments *George Spoor*
1952	First public showing of Cinerama: a three projector, three-screen process *Fred Waller* First extensive use of stereophonic sound *Hazard Reeves*
1953	First public showing of CinemaScope: *The Robe* (NOTE: Director of Photography was Leon Shamroy) *Dr Henri Chrétien*
1955	First public showing of Todd-AO: *Oklahoma!* *Dr Brian O'Brien* First use of six high-fidelity sound channels on one strip of film *Fred Hynes*

Todd-AO is revolutionary even for an industry accustomed to frequent, sudden changes. "Todd-AO," according to Arthur Knight in *The Liveliest Art* (Macmillan, 1957, p 322), "fills the widest of wide screens with a clean, sparkling picture that is far brighter and better defined than anything possible in the 35mm . . . systems." "Todd-AO," in the opinion of critic Dick Williams (The Los Angeles Mirror-News, 19 November 1955), "achieves a new peak in high-fidelity sound, color photography and feeling of audience participation . . . the best process to come along."

The name, Todd-AO, is more significant than it would seem to be at first glance. For both the system and, representatively, its name comprise two of the most essential elements of a motion picture: showmanship and technical excellence.* The late Michael Todd assuredly was one of *the* great showmen of our time. AO symbolizes one of the oldest and finest optical laboratories in the United States, the American Optical company.

The conceptual basis of the Todd-AO motion picture system is the one hundred twenty-eight degree lens. It was developed, shortly after World War II, for the purpose of training Navy jet pilots. The other lenses, designed to make Todd-AO a flexible and thus a practical narrative medium, came into being in 1953. Necessarily, the projector, developed the following year by the Philips Company of The Netherlands, contains equally up-to-date principles. Todd-AO, therefore, among all the -Ramas, -Scopes and -Visions, is the one truly *new* major scientific development in motion pictures since the advent of sound.

—Albert Teichner

*A third essential element, not represented, could be termed 'corporate means'—through which an idea was developed into reality. The men responsible for this element bear two of the most respected names in the business history of motion pictures: Joseph M Schenck and George P Skouras.

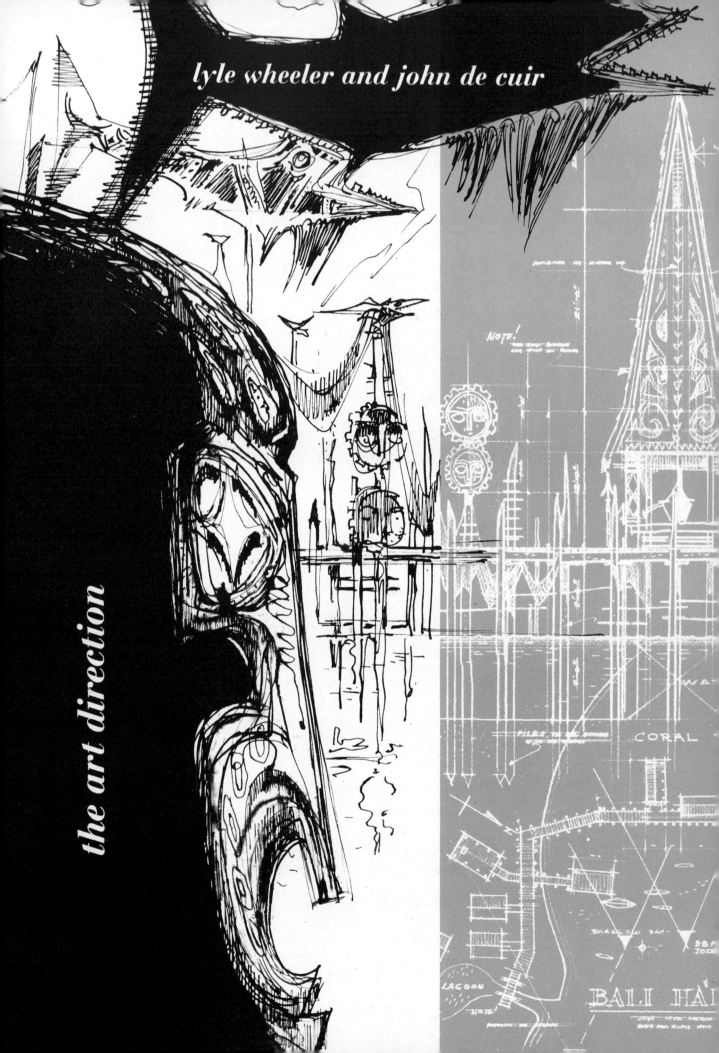

lyle wheeler and john de cuir

the art direction

walter scott and paul fox

set decorations

the costumes dorothy jeakins

WHITE HAWK IDOL

LENEVHEV

MONOLITHS

NA-AMEL

IDOL

NAHBWILAGHAI LOG GONGS

CHIEFS ANCESTOR IMAGES - TABOO SIGNS

BOAR TUSKERS SHRINE

COVERED (BOO HUT)

BOAR TUSK BONE

TOM TOMS

HARD PACKED RED EARTH

KRAAL

DJ

THE "MAKI"

MALEKULA DANCE (NEW HEBRIDES)

C - CHIEF
S - SUB CHIEF (MEDICINE MAN)

W - WHIP MAN
A - ASHMEN
T - FIRE TENDERS
M - BIRD MEN
V - VARUS (BEATERS)
B - "BLUE BOYS" (HEAD HUNTERS)
O - OTNELLAS (MUSICIANS)
F - "FLOWER GIRLS"
G - "GRASS GIRLS"

the production .....

BIG

A CAMERA

TODD·AO

COSTUMES
AND DANCERS

AND MORE ACTORS

SOME
... ART...

SOME PROPS

SOME ACTORS

AND MUSIC

SPECIAL EFFECTS

AND THEN WE GOT AN ISLAND....

HEADS — OF HEADS — IN THE CLOUDS —

Dick Rodgers

Oscar Hammerstein, George Skouras, & Josh

VIPs

Location Set

Mrs. Birkmyre, owner of the beautiful 'de Becque' estate,

with Mitzi

Leon Shamroy, Josh, & Buddy Adler

HERE WE ARE   BEHIND THE SCENES ...

Rossano

Ray & John: The Brain Trust

... France: *La Sirène*

Frank McArdle, grip best boy
(best boy=asst)

Al Parker, grip (i e, carpenter
& general aide)

BOYS WILL   BE   BOYS

AND GIRLS   WLLL BE GIRLS — H m m —

Jan Hanrahan

Beverly Johnson

Muffett Webb

May Fewell

'Nellie'

Frank Gilley, grip, operating camera dolly

WORKING "ON SCHED" — YOU CAN SEE WHAT THAT MEANS...

REARLY HAVE

SO HARD — !

Jim Cane, drapery man,
is up there—somewhere!

WE WORKED

Clyde Taylor, juicer (i e, lamp op) & friend

Bob Henderson & Fred Hall, best boy & gaffer
(i e, asst & head electrician)

John, & Modest Mickey
Sherrard, wardrobe

Hugh Crawford, asst
cameraman, assisting

Joe Kane, sound
mixer

Orik Barrett,
boom man, &
'Cable'

Mik
a

Mushy Harmell
2nd asst dir

Ben Kadish, asst dir

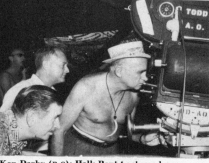

Ken Darby (B G); Hall; Paul Lockwood, cam op
with Leon

Musical Run-through

Bill Jurgenson
working clap

Reeder Boss,
wardrobe

Harold Bavaird, playback op

Mrs Shamroy
(Mary Anderson)

Dorothy Jeakins
costumes

WHY'RE YOU
SO SHY
DOTTIE...?!

Miss O Skouras,
Mrs Hammerstein

Mrs Leatherbee, Josh's sister
with Buddy

PLANS AND REHEARSALS, SCRIPT CHANGES AND TESTS...

Key grip Leo McCreary

GETTING A FIRM
GRIP ON THE
POLITICAL SITUATION

Construction Crew

Warren Hsieh

Candace Lee

Advance Unit

'Liat;' the brothers Crawford

Script Rehearsal

Joe Curtis, & 'Prof,' 'Stewpot,' 'Billis,' 'sailors'

Mrs Adler
(Anita Louise)

Mrs Logan

reary, &
Bill Reynolds, prod asst

Skip Sanford
Todd-AO rep

Special Effects Unit

Don Nobles, effects' props; Kenny Williams, effects'
cam op; others

Mrs Brazzi

PLUS BUILDING AND MOVING... MAKE FOR FEW RESTS...

2nd Unit

NO COMMENT —

Stan Cortez, cam; Ray Kellogg, dir

Marshall Wolins, script clerk

THE RAIN IN KAUAI

FALLS MAINLY FROM THE SKY-AI

'Nurses'

Mary Jo Flanders, Phyllis Butcher, Anna James,
Jane Lucas

Machado, grip, sporting one of his daily-different hats

'Bloody Mary' —
looking anything *but*

'Ngana' & 'Jerome'

Kadish & costumed fri

'Capt Brackett'

'Adams' & 'Harbison' with 'Er

Dorothy & John — filling in
some *extra* time

Dale

Thana

The Bookmakers . . .

STILL WE

ALWAYS FOUND TIME, HERE AND THERE, FOR SOME FUN...

Jim Mitchell
photographer

OUR OWN MICHENER
BOB MAYER AND HIS OWN MISAYE

Leroy Prinz, choreographer;
Archie Savage, 'chief' dancer

Red Crawford, asst cam,
measuring *starlight*

John, & Bill Buell, makeup man

Mitzi, & Helen Turpin
hair stylist

Studio Set

John de Cuir
art dir

VIPs

Producer, cinematographer, director

Walter Scott
head set dec

Paul Fox
set dec

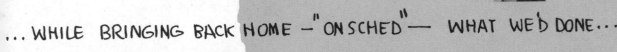

...WHILE BRINGING BACK HOME —"ON SCHED"— WHAT WE'D DONE...

Lyle Wheeler
head of art de

BACK TO THE STUDIO — FOR SOME....

DUBBING

SCORING

SOUTH PACIFIC

THE PERFECT SHOW IN TODD-AO

SOME PUBLICITY...

rossano brazzi

"By accident," is the way Rossano Brazzi describes the start of a career that, to date, adds up to roles in 88 films—made in seven countries—and 200 plays. Already celebrated throughout Europe for his award-winning performances, he has become familiar to the American public since such movies as *Summertime, The Barefoot Contessa* and *Three Coins in the Fountain.* Yet, despite an incredibly active career, Rossano has managed to lead an equally full life outside the theatre. Though married (to Lidia Bertolini, renowned and beloved for her unerring sense of humor) and studying civil law at the University of Florence, he still found time to compete in national swimming meets, play professional football (European variety) and win boxing and tennis championships. During the war, he received a commendation from the American High Command for his underground resistance work. A twentieth century man of Renaissance mold—Italian Renaissance, of course—Rossano has tried many things, from mastering five languages to practising gourmet 'chefmanship,' and has done all of them well.

"Emile is not a man of compromise. A serious man, strong, knowing life but with ideals, he is forty years old when he finds his love—an American nurse from a different culture, a different generation. For his Polynesian wife, dead, he felt much affection. He was alone. But I think that this is the first time Emile de Becque is in love."

John Kerr is a new type of film actor. An introvert by nature, an extrovert by profession, he combines courtesy and charm with cynicism and indifference. The son of actress June Walker and Geoffrey Kerr the British writer, he studied English Literature at Harvard and, until recently, was engaged in obtaining a master's degree in Russian Literature from Columbia University. A devoted at-homer, John is an enthusiast of 18th century music, chess, his home workshop and tennis. Yet, from his Cape Playhouse debut at the age of ten—his happiest experience: appearing with Gertrude Lawrence in *O Mistress Mine* (1948)—he has always given his greatest attention to the theatre. His first Broadway appearance, in *Bernardine*, won him immediate recognition and the role that co-starred him with Deborah Kerr in *Tea and Sympathy. Tea and Sympathy* brought him to Hollywood . . . and to *SOUTH PACIFIC.*

john kerr

"I have a feeling that Joe Cable would be one of the misplaced after the war. He comes from a nice, unneurotic background—safe, secure, a little remote. It hadn't prepared him for the Marines, much less becoming a good killer—he's been in combat. . . .What he goes through exposes his humanity. He's always been a serious person; he tries to see the world clearly. But, before, his world was a great deal smaller."

mitzi gaynor

When Mitzi Gaynor was offered the part of Nellie Forbush, many in Hollywood had misgivings. She had always been cast in backstage musicals, usually as a happily naive chorine. Now the question was: could she act? Sing? Yes. Dance? Definitely. But act? Who knew? Yet Josh Logan was so sure of her ability he offered the role to no one else! That he was right should not come as a surprise to anyone who knows her. A veteran of 1,000 hours of USO entertainment, Mitzi made her stage debut at 14 with the Los Angeles Light Opera Company. *My Blue Heaven* was her first film and *Golden Girl,* made the following year, confirmed her position as a rising young star. But a long series of rising-young-star-type pictures brought her no closer to her goal of Actress and a great deal closer to utter frustration. THEN Mitzi made up her mind! With the help of husband Jack Bean she would unlearn all her 'Gaynorisms' (her word) and just be herself. Result: a charming, warm-hearted, high-spirited girl—the ideal Nellie.

"Nellie's not really mature. When difficult situations pop up she's very flat-footed and says exactly what's in her mind. When she tries to cover up it's a disaster. She's very loving and she wants to be loved."

france nuyen

France Nuyen comes to the role of Liat with a special understanding of what happens when two vastly different cultures meet. Daughter of an Indo-Chinese seaman and a French mother, she has had a cosmopolitan background that belies her eighteen years. At the Beaux Arts School in Marseilles where she studied, painters immediately noticed her exceptional beauty and her first money was earned as an artists' model, followed by more lucrative assignments in advertising photography. When she came to New York in 1957 with her mother, however, she had less luck in finding modelling work and had to settle for a job in a cookie shop—with expected results to her figure. An *un*expected audition before Oscar Hammerstein soon solved that problem.

"Liat is innocent—very child-like, timid. She does not know experience, only nature. After, she knows one thing: she love the man. She is very pure and—confidence? how do you say? —she trusts everybody."

Ray Walston succeeded the hard way. Born in New Orleans, he went to work at an early age, setting aside dreams of an acting career. His first job was in printing. His second: a financial reporter on the Item-Tribune. Later he moved to Houston. Margo Jones, director of the Houston Community Playhouse, was then seeking someone for a one-line part in *High Tor* and Ray's career was launched. After nine years at the Houston and Cleveland Playhouses he came East, working intermittently as a linotypist until his performances started to attract critical interest. In 1949 he won the New York Critics' Best Supporting Actor award for his work in *Summer and Smoke*. His next big part was Luther Billis in the road and London companies of *SOUTH PACIFIC*, a part to which he now returns after two years as the Devil in *Damn Yankees*.

"To me Billis is a very understanding guy *first* of all. People usually label him: the con man, the big operator. But look at him with Nellie—unselfishly, honestly concerned about her, protective. Billis is a real human being."

ray walston

Russ Brown is the only living actor to have worked for four generations of Hammersteins. His first job was singing in a nickelodeon, an activity strongly disapproved of by his father. Running away from home in 1912 (aged 15), he got a job in a musical comedy. Later he joined Bert Wheeler —first of his vaudeville duos. Since then Russ has appeared in hundreds of shows across the country, on stage and over the air. From the *SOUTH PACIFIC* road company he went to *Damn Yankees*. Now he returns to his old role: George Brackett, Captain, USN.

Jack Mullaney worked double shifts in a Cincinnati watch factory to earn enough for drama training in New York. Three years later he had $1,000 . . . and a notice from his draft board! Two years later he had his discharge and a ticket to New York. But before Jack could take one acting lesson, he found himself replacing the late James Dean on Philco Playhouse. Immediately afterwards he was cast as the minister in *The Remarkable Mr Pennypacker*. After 100 television shows and three films, Jack is endowed with another doctorate (in name, anyway) as the Professor.

Ken Clark bulldozed his way into films. Literally! He was driving a bulldozer, after a two-year Coast Guard stint in the Pacific, when a stranger offered him a screen test. Suspicious, Ken turned it down. Months later, fume-choked, rain-soaked, deafened, he "suddenly climbed off that 'dozer and quit." Applying, without hope, for the screen test, he was grabbed by the 'opposition' for a role on Climax. Ken made six films in eighteen months and had completed his fifteenth television lead when Josh Logan called him to play Stewpot.

As Juanita Hall sees it now, she was the brashest of fourteen year olds, trying for the chorus of the original *Show Boat* production. Luck was with her, though, and a year in that famous company supplied an invaluable education in the musical stage, as did two following years in *Green Pastures*. By 1933 Juanita was sufficiently versed in theatrecraft to direct Hall Johnson's play *Run, Little Chillun'* and form her own choral group. Through the late '30's the Juanita Hall Choir gave over 5,000 concerts. By 1942 she was back on the stage, with the Lunts in *The Pirate*. Much radio work followed but 1947-48 "a period of great bad luck" found her living close to poverty. *SOUTH PACIFIC* changed all that and she has moved from one triumph to another since first stepping out on the stage as Bloody Mary.

juanita hall

"Bloody Mary is a very loving mother. She has an inner quality—she *knows* when something's right. She's smart but not conniving. Her comedy isn't really a part of her. She's a woman brought up close to the soil who is wise in the ways of nature."

Floyd Simmons was a celebrity before he ever had a screen credit. A star athlete, in both 1948 and 1952 he scored third in the decathlon, the Olympic Games' highest competition. He competed against the great Harrison Dillard in the high hurdles and played for North Carolina in the Sugar Bowl. This despite a Purple Heart received when he was not quite 19. Floyd left sports for commercial art but soon moved into a different sort of Studio. Being signed to star in a new television series is the immediate result of his portrayal of Commander Bill Harbison, USNR.

Tom Laughlin, onetime halfback in the Big Ten Conference, turned to acting when a shattered shoulder kept him out of pro football. After a year of intensive drama studies with the famous Father Walsh at Marquette University, he founded his own Little Theatre group. But its projects were more successful artistically than financially. So Tom headed for California. Ten days after arriving he got his first television job on Climax. A veteran of several dozen television shows and three films, he has his most important role to date: Lieutenant Bus Adams, USNAF.

Candace Lee, eight years old, has already appeared in five films: *Love is a Many-Splendored Thing*, *The King and I*, etc , and in two major television productions: *Child of the Regiment* and *The Family Nobody Wanted*. For various roles she learned Japanese, Siamese, Spanish and Chinese. So, what does Ngana speak? French!

Warren Hsieh, remembered as the youngest son of Yul Brynner in *The King and I*, is a trouper at six who has had twelve film and television roles. He played with John Wayne, the late Humphrey Bogart, and Tyrone Power. Then, in *China Gate*, he grew up—as an *actor*. In every other way, he's still a wonderful little boy . . . our Jerome.

other views.....

rodgers and hammerstein

The King and I
Carousel
Oklahoma!
State Fair

joshua logan

Sayonara
Picnic
Bus Stop*
Mr Roberts

buddy adler

A Hatful of Rain
Heaven Knows, Mr Allison
Anastasia
*Bus Stop
Love is a Many-Splendored Thing
From Here to Eternity
                    and others

VIPs

the means .....

.....the end

George P Skouras, President, MAGNA

south pacific's "winners"

the perfect show in todd-ao!

THE CREATORS . . .

presentation:	rodgers & hammerstein
score:	richard rodgers
lyrics:	oscar hammerstein II
direction:	joshua logan
production:	buddy adler
photography:	leon shamroy
music direction:	alfred newman
vocal direction:	ken darby
art direction:	lyle wheeler
	john de cuir
set decoration:	walter scott
	paul fox
screenplay:	paul osborn

from the musical stageplay SOUTH PACIFIC:

richard rodgers
oscar hammerstein II

from the book TALES OF THE SOUTH PACIFIC:

james a michener

(originally produced on the stage by richard rodgers,
oscar hammerstein II, joshua logan and leland hayward)

BTC choreography:	leroy prinz
costume designs:	dorothy jeakins
makeup:	ben nye
hair styles:	helen turpin

THE ENHANCERS . . .

wardrobe mgrs:	reeder boss
	norma brown
assts:	mickey sh
	dale hend
makeup artists:	allan snyder
	bill buell
body makeup:	bunny gar
hairdressers:	marie walter
	buddy king

THE AIDES . . .

asst director:	
2nd assts:	
dialogue coach:	
script clerk	
production asst:	
unit prod mg	
prod researchers	
prod publici	
asst cameraman:	
2nd assts:	
camera operator:	
asst (mechan	
art dirs' illustr	
continuity ar	
matte artists	

THE ORCHESTRATORS . . .

film:	edward powell
	pete king
	bernard mayers
stage (original):	robert russell bennett

THE BUILDERS . . .

set specifications:	george dudley
coordinator:	walter ledgerwood
construction foreman:	loren woods
plasterers:	james stephens
	robert thompson
painters:	harvey jackson
	john lowess
landscapers:	george novak
	peter rea
	joe fisher
drapery men:	james cane
	charles long
prop makers:	paul skelton
	walter de hart